THE ORIGIN OF WOUNDS

THE ANHINGA PRIZE FOR POETRY

1983
Ricardo Pau-Llosa
Sorting Metaphors

1984
Sherry Rind
The Hawk in the Backyard

1985
Judith Kitchen
Perennials

1986
Robert Levy
The Whistle Maker

1987
Will Wells
Conversing with the Light

1988
Julianne Seeman
Enough Light to See

1989
Nick Bozanic
The Long Drive Home

1991
Jean Monahan
Hands

1992
Earl S. Braggs
Hat Dancer Blue

1993
Janet Holmes
The Physicist at the Mall

1994
Frank X. Gaspar
*Mass for the Grace
of a Happy Death*

1995
Ann Neelon
Easter Vigil

1996
Keith Ratzlaff
Man Under a Pear Tree

1997
Michele Wolf
Conversations During Sleep

1998
Julia B. Levine
Practicing for Heaven

1999
Kathleen Wakefield
Notations on the Visible World

2000
Ruth L. Schwartz
Singular Bodies

2001
Patti White
Tackle Box

2002
Erika Meitner
*Inventory
at the All-night Drugstore*

2003
Deborah Landau
Orchidelirium

2004
Joshua Poteat
Ornithologies

2005
Sandy Longhorn
Blood Almanac

2006
Meredith Walters
All you have to do is ask

2007
Kenneth Hart
Uh Oh Time

2008
Rhett Iseman Trull
The Real Warnings

2009
Gretchen Steele Pratt
One Island

2010
Kimberly Burwick
Horses in the Cathedral

2011
Rosalynde Vas Dias
Only Blue Body

2012
Anna Ross
If a Storm

2013
Bethany Schultz +Hurst
Miss Lost Nation

2014
Robin Beth Schaer
Shipbreaking

2015
Elizabeth A.I. Powell
*Willy Loman's
Reckless Daughter*

2016
Hautie
*To Whitey
& the Cracker Jack*

2017
Joaquin Zihuatanejo
Arsonist

2018
Heidi Reszies
*Of Water
and Other Soft Constructions*

2019
Caronae Howell
Index for September 11th

2020
Clemonce Heard
Tragic City

2021
Craig Beaven
*Teaching the Baby
to Say I Love You*

2022
Katie Fuller
Careful

2023
Julie Marie Wade
Quick Change Artist

2024
Rasaq Malik Gbolahan
The Origin of Wounds

THE ORIGIN OF WOUNDS

RASAQ MALIK GBOLAHAN

2024 Anhinga Prize For Poetry
Selected by Kaveh Bassiri

ANHINGA PRESS
TALLAHASSEE, FLORIDA 2025

Copyright © Rasaq Malik Gbolahan All rights reserved under
International and Pan-American Copyright Conventions.

No portion of this book may be reproduced in any form without the written permission of the publisher, except by a reviewer, who may quote brief passages in connection with a review for a magazine or newspaper.

Cover art: *Let's Be Kids,* Photograph by Rubie Okpara, Nigeria, 2025
Cover design: Jay Snodgrass
Author photograph: Santi Femi
Text design and production: Carol Lynne Knight

Type Styles: Poem texts are set in Garamond Premier Pro. Adobe designer Robert Slimbach based the design of Garamond Premier Pro on his study of the collection of Claude Garamond's metal punches and type designs at the Plantin-Moretus Museum in Antwerp, Belgium. Garamond, a French punchcutter, produced a refined array of book types in the mid-1500s that combined an unprecedented degree of balance and elegance. Titles are set in Yana designed by Laura Worthington. She published her first typeface in 2010 and now has more than 200 type designs.

Library of Congress Cataloging-in-Publication Data
The Origin of Wounds by Rasaq Malik Gbolahan, First Edition
ISBN – 978-1-934695-94-4
Library of Congress Cataloging Card Number – 2025944952

Founded in 1974, Anhinga Press Inc. is dedicated wholly to the
publication and appreciation of fine poetry and other literary genres.

For personal orders, catalogs and information write to:
Anhinga Press
P.O. Box 3665
Tallahassee, Florida 32315
Website: www.anhingapress.org
Email: info@anhinga.org

Published in the United States
by Anhinga Press
Tallahassee, Florida
First Edition, 2025

For
My Mother, Father, and Umm Bilal

For
Jumoke Verissimo

For
Homeland

ANHINGA PRESS ADVISORY BOARD

Our thanks to these wonderful poets
for supporting the mission of Anhinga Press —
to publish fine poetry.

Ellen Bass
Richard Blanco
Rick Campbell
Terri Carrion
Denise Duhamel
Dorianne Laux
Naomi Shihab Nye
Virgil Suarez
Terese Svoboda

Carol Lynne Knight, Co-director
Kristine Snodgrass, Co-director
Karla Van Vliet, Co-director
Amber Lunderman, Assistant Editor

ANHINGA PRESS BOARD OF DIRECTORS

Sue Scavo, President
Michael Trammell, Secretary
Craig Beaven, Director
Rafael Gamero, Director
Jennifer Schomburg Kanke, Director
Carlos Miranda, Director
Elizabeth A.I. Powell, Director

CONTENTS

Introduction   ix

Acknowledgments   xi

I.

Biography of Homeland   3

Holy are your 99 Names, Lord   5

A Ledger of Losses   7

After the Blasts   10

The Weight of Leaving   12

What They Remember   15

Ghazal: Moon   18

Darak   20

II.

What Crosses the Sea   25

Requiem at Sea I   27

Elegy for the Drowned   29

Doors   31

Requiem at Sea II   33

Hunger   35

The Grief that Startles the Waters   37

III.

Mercy   41

The Origin of Wounds   42

God   44

All Around Me   46

In Praise of the End   47

Elegy I   49

Blessed Be the Body in Death   51

Elegy II   53

Months After My Grandfather's Death   55

Guide to Visiting the Dead   57

IV.

Emptiness   61

To Return to This Land   63

Dusk, Again   67

Coffins   70

Ghazal: Ruins   71

What Remains   72

Bury Us   74

Ode to Last Wishes   76

In Praise of the World   78

Notes   80

About the Author   82

INTRODUCTION

These poems from Rasaq Malik Gbolahan ensue from a patient but deeply felt understanding of the human condition and of what wounds are. At once contemporary and runic, they confront us with lives as observed through a poet's eye. There are all manner of wounds here — of home and exile, of filial bonds broken, of wars and rumors of war, of shattered intimate dreams. A resolute poet, not given to superciliousness or half measures, Malik insists on seeing things through in a meditative vein. We become intimate with injuries and the injured. We even glimpse the perpetrators sometimes but the poetry is such that our sympathies lie, always, with the wounded. Malik's power as a poet derives largely from his ability to elicit visions of our individual and collective losses — and his consciousness in presenting us with irreducible, inexterminable hope. It is as if he unconsciously heeds the adjuration in the Yorùbá language that says we must insist on seeing even when weeping. We see in these poems what wounds birth, what they touch, what they take away, and what they transform. Malik has long concerned himself in his practice as a poet with the craft of stating without understating or overstating. Here, his transformation of the ode into the 21st century is proof that in the hands of a true poet, nothing goes to waste. Not even wounds, and wounding. There is nothing the poet cannot transmute.

In this collection, the poet does not look away and he does not flinch. The reader is presented with a portrait of pain so palpable that we can still feel the pulse if we care enough to check. The poems here unlatch, with stoic diligence, a host of windows and doors into the turmoil and torment of the most vulnerable among us. Malik concerns himself with all manner of injuries and what they leave behind. In what is heard, and what is overheard between the lines, we learn about ourselves and our need for resilience and redemption.

It is a brave poet indeed who makes his subject a primal problem. They are braver still who probe into beginnings, origins. But herein lies the challenge for Malik whose working canvas is local and concomitantly global. More than noun or verb, more than the present or the merely historic, this gifted poet delves way beyond the etymology of the wound into its very genealogy. As it happens, "wound" in any language, often falls into the narrow category of words from prehistory. In English, we trace its ancestry right into the linguistic fog of proto-Germanic speech as "wundian" and there we are one with all others who started their respective journeys from any of the 7,000 languages in active or passive use on the planet.

Malik is the guide you want to go with in that liminal world of the blinding fog of wounds because he knows the difference between flesh wounds and mortal wounds. His lines keep the consciousness on the consequences of wounds without losing sight of the balm of hope or the recuperative and restorative powers of time. If we listen close, we learn to avoid self-inflicted wounds or paths that lead to constrictor wounds.

Long practice has made Malik a master of the dirge as a genre. His delivery seems almost effortless but then we also know that there is really no such thing as effortlessness in any genre. Before we get halfway in the collection, we realize that we are watching and listening to a master at work. When he applies his pen to the fate of children, infants — literally the 'unspeaking ones' — whose only form of protest is the cry, he makes their anguish eloquent. In this collection, Malik makes the grieving world around us audible, legible and tactile — such is the power of his gift. It is for a reason — so we may birth healers and not killers.

The poems here are commemorative in a way that newspaper reportage can never be. They flow from a wellspring that is deeper than the news cycle and they burn with feeling. From origins of wounds through grief and grieving to the lingering shadows and echoes of sorrow, the audience is taken to a place before wounds and given a glimpse of a world without wounds.

Because his poetry is a peculiar fusion of language and musicality, the reader is guided into the lived and spent lives of the majority of those the poet writes and sings about. The cadences that the poet deploys in his odes are ethereal, fully plumbing the emotions of the reader. His metaphors are aural miracles of language, turned just so that we do not fail to recognize an inflection in the rendition, but not so much that the gravity of the message is lost to verbal showmanship. The musicality of his lines, measured and fluid, mirror the landscape he has labored to paint for us from the very first word in the volume to the last.

This collection is a triumph of feeling and form. It is also a triumph of control in a genre of poetry in which it is easiest to go overboard. Malik's final gift to the wounded is the dignity he offers in the face of gargantuan suffering. To hear the lament raised without stridency, the names of the departed as the angels would pronounce them, is a gift not of this world. Comfort lies in this fact, and in this solace the ultimate triumph of the ineffable. We give thanks for divine gifts such as Malik has brought us.

— Tade Ipadeola, author of *The Sahara Testaments.*

ACKNOWLEDGMENTS

Immense gratitude to editors of journals where these poems or previous versions of them first appeared:
Michigan Quarterly Review: "Blessed Be the Body in Death"
Nimrod International: "Hunger"
Notre Dame Review: "Dusk, Again"
Poetry International: "The Weight of Leaving" published as "Exit"
Porter House Review: "To Return to this Land"
Transition: "What Crosses the Sea," "The Grief that Startles the Waters" and "Requiem at Sea 1"
The Nation: "Darak" published as "Siege"

Thank you to friends and families whose constant prayers and support continue to anchor my literary journey. Thanks to Prof. Kwame Dawes for playing the pivotal role of an African literary grandfather. Thanks to Drs. Tosin Gbogi, Jumoke Verissimo, Shola Adenekan, James Yékú, and Soji Cole for being my guiding lights.

Thanks to Aunty Tosin for being my literary light at Blue Crescent International College, Iseyin. Thanks to Ojo Adeshina, Awaal Gata, Jalaludeen Ibrahim, Yax Mokwa, and Michael Loveth for trusting my poems enough to offer me a space when I needed it. Thank you to Laura Kaminski. Dear Laura, you did create amazing poets out of your unbridled generosity. Thanks for sending books to all of us who continue to carry your name with us. Thank you to Sara Perkins and Akin Omokemi. I am so grateful for the love and support over the years. Sara, I continue to treasure those books.

Immense gratitude to Danusha Laméris. Thanks for sending your debut collection to Nigeria when I requested it in 2015. Thanks for the autograph and the precious letter. Thank you for your continuous belief in my work. I am eternally grateful. Thank you to Baba Khaled Mattawa for extending his unrestrained support to me. May Allah reward you abundantly in this dunya and akhirah. Aameen.

Also, a legion of thanks to 'Gbenga Adeoba, Olajide Salawu, Hussain Ahmed, Chinua Ezenwa-Ohaeto, O-Jeremiah Agbaakin, Ber Anena, Elliott Uguru, Tryphena Yeboah, Uche Okonkwo, Zainab Omaki, Abraham Kedong, Alina Nguyen, Caleb Petersen, Chibueze Darlington, Emmanuel Dairo, Rahaman Abiola Toheeb, Busayo Olatunde, Adedayo Agarau, Salim Yunusa, Oladosu Tunde, Arasi Kamolideen, Adewale Oreshade, Adeshina Raphael, S.A. Ibrahim, Ayobami Kayode, Olaniyi Waheed, Tolulope Oke, Osieka Osinimu Alao, Atolagbe Segun, Ojo Abayomi, Muideen Adekunle, Olu Aribisala, Dami Ajayi, Oseni Ibrahim, Ibrahim Odugbemi, Alexander Olomo, Ba Sabouke, Folorunso Fatai Adisa, Abubakar Ibrahim, Seun Williams, Fasasi Rosheed Oladipupo, Amina Akinola Bamidele, Afeez Sholanke, Damilare Bello, Kawthar Babatunde, Santi Femi, Ifesinachi Nwadike, Ndubuisi Martins, Badiu Akinola Akinbode, Elufowora Eluyemi, Daud Abiola,

Hussein Abdulbasit, Lanase Hussein, Lateef Rahmon Kehinde, Musediq Adekunle Fajimi, Adegoke Mutiu Bolade, Muhammad Abass-Giwa, Ghiyathudeen Alharaky Oyelayo, Ibraheem Olanrewaju Dauda, and Taofeek Ibrahim Adeshina.

Thank you, Nasiba Babale. Thanks for holding my poems close to your heart. For sharing my words in places I have never walked. Thank you for inviting me to the Kano International Poetry Festival. Thanks to Servio Gbadamosi and Femi Morgan for granting me the stage at Atmosphere. Thanks to Tohib Adejumo and Sahid Adejumo for inviting me to Memphis and for their support of my craft. Mo dupe pupo.

A massive thanks to Oredola Ibrahim. Thanks for being more than a friend for more than a decade. Thanks for your devotion to Atelewo, and for being the powerhouse of that initiative that continues to rejuvenate the Yorùbá language and literature. Thanks to all the teachers that have taught me, all the teachers whose words gifted me a lifetime of language. Thanks to Prof. Ramonu Sanusi for inviting me to contribute to an anthology years ago. Thanks for believing in my work, Prof.

Thanks to Baba Sulaiman Kamordeen Araoyo for supporting my work. Thanks to Prof. Saheed Aderinto for his words of encouragement. Thanks to Baba Tade Ipadeola for writing this engaging introduction. Thanks to all the places where I have performed my poems. Thanks to all the people that invited me to read and perform my poems at the University of Ibadan. Thanks to the directors of plays where my voice found a home. Thanks to Baba Yemi Akintokun, Uncle Biodun, and all the faces that witnessed my performances and said prayers. Thanks to all the classrooms where my poems once graced the attentive ears of listeners.

To my departed beloveds: Mommy Morning Star, Mommy Gbenga, Abiodun Ridwan, Brother Abideen, Abdul Rahaman Rufai, Islamiyyah, Opoola Tunde, Aunty Ope, and all those whose memories I return to. Thank you.

Thanks to Kaveh Bassiri for selecting this manuscript, and thanks to Anhinga Press for the care and love.

To you, dear readers, I hope you find something dear to hold to your heart when you read this book. Shukran.

THE ORIGIN OF WOUNDS

I.

Yesterday I lost a country.
I was in a hurry,
and didn't notice when it fell from me
like a broken branch from a forgetful tree.
— Dunya Mikhail

I wish the children didn't die.
I wish they would be temporarily elevated
to the skies until the war ends.
— Ghassan Kanafani

For a decade and a half now, Nigeria has been at war with violent extremists, a war that has directly and indirectly cost the lives of nearly 350,000 people. It started when a group that came to be known as Boko Haram started radicalising people in the early 2000s and later decided to forcefully carve out parts of the country to establish a caliphate. Boko Haram has since splintered, leading to the establishment of two other terror groups, the Islamic State West Africa Province (ISWAP) and Ansaru, both having strong links with international jihadist networks. Many years into the insurgency, the authorities still struggle to restore peace to the region.

— Kunle Adebajo, "The Fight Against Boko Haram Leaves a Trail of Ruin and Ashes," *HumAngle,* April 1, 2024.

BIOGRAPHY OF HOMELAND

       i.

I begin where the map opens into wounds that open into rooms
  where the children wake up each morning uncertain of their safety,

unsure of when the sky will be bright enough for them to see birds
   in place of bullets. I begin where the hands of a clock cease,

the hands of war reversing, returning us to the streets of villages
    where there are people counting their dead and searching

for their missing beloveds. Some nights, the children ask
    their parents about *the time the war will stop*. But in these

villages there are no clocks without their hands ceased. No one knows
    when bullets will stop crowding the air, when bombs

will stop dropping on buildings occupied by children whose dreams
    are fragile in this land where no one knows when the hands of war

will stop demolishing the buildings, rendering families homeless,
   displaced; pushing them to borders, to places where they will watch

each day end without their beloveds.

       ii.

   I begin with the blood-stained flag of my homeland
     wrapped around a casket that contains
       the remains of a child.

   I begin where the earth quivers beneath the feet of children,
     where the croons of birds
      fade in the din of bullets.

  I know the weight of silence clogging
   the air in places where there are mass graves.

      I know where history bleeds:
     In 1967, the civil war began in my country.
   Decades later, the bones of the dead still groan
    beneath the earth of this country where
      the dead never sleep.

  iii.

The dead never sleep. In my country,
  there are unmarked graves of patriots whose names

my country never remembers because no one remembers
  all the names of the dead in a country where death lurks

in the eyes of everyone waking up to see houses
   reduced to debris. Today in Baga,

Aisha is burying her child and she is reciting إنالله وينالله راجعون
 as she lowers her remains into the earth of this country

where nothing blooms, where nothing carries the torch of hope
    because there are days when the natives weigh their dreams

on the scale of war. *Displaced,* they call those who flee home
   amidst unrest. *Immigrants,* they call those who carry

the wounds of homeland to a foreign country.

  iv.

On nights of curfews, there are people
    panicking in rooms where nothing promises
     them a day bereft of soldiers
       brandishing guns in their streets.

   Today, there is no one to call the *adhan*.
    There are loved ones grieving their dead

whose hands will never hold again the blood-soaked flag of this land
   where everything aches for a memorial.

HOLY ARE YOUR 99 NAMES, LORD

        i.

Today, the map of my country unfurls into besieged villages, Lord.
In every room, there are mothers supplicating for their children, Lord.

Outside, gunshots unsettle the air, startle the birds to flee their nests.
In every room, there are fathers praying for your mercy, Lord.

Some days, there are bodies surrounded by a wake of vultures in the streets.
The bodies belong to those left unburied after nights of blasts, Lord.

        ii.

Holy are your 99 names on days when bullets do not rend
the soft bones of the children and their mothers do not grieve, Lord.

Holy are nights bereft of drones carrying grenades in the sky
and holy are mornings when birds flap their wings to praise you, Lord.

Holy are the streets of this land without coffins named after the children
and holy is the flag of this land waving in the air undarkened with smoke, Lord.

Holy are days when the children play football,
pick daisies, and catch grasshoppers, Lord.

Holy are the children and their parents lifting their voices into the air,
reciting your 99 names before missiles split the walls of the *masjid,* Lord.

        iii.

In Arabic, the word for holy is مُقَدَّس.
   Holy is the hand of a woman without a shawl of blood, Lord.

But tonight, there is a woman mopping the blood
   of her child in Gwoza, and there is a dying lantern in a room of mourning, Lord.

There are no hymns of love in this cathedral of loss
   because this land burns and there is no water to douse it, Lord.

iv.

Holy is the poem without grief,
    but there is grief enveloping this poem, Lord.

There is fear embroidering this poem,
    and there is despair moving through these lines, Lord.

There is nothing holy about a world where the headlines
    of newspapers begin with *the children are massacred,* Lord.

v.

There is nothing holy about people counting losses,
    summing their dead, burying their remains, Lord.

Holy are your 99 names, and holy are the children in their rooms
    across the world, praying for the deluge of your mercy, Lord.

Holy will be this world, if only the children are unharmed,
    safe, happy, and no one has to flee their homeland, Lord.

A LEDGER OF LOSSES

The casualties are not only those who started
A fire and now cannot put out. Thousands
Are burning that have no say in the matter.
— J.P. Clark's *The Casualties*

    i.

In the history of my homeland,
          It's 1967.

In the field of a razed town, a woman kneels to bury her child.
She holds a shovel, scrapes the earth, pours dirt, slowly,
into the small grave of her child. She shovels dirt, slowly,
into the small grave that contains her child.

        No one hears the sound of her grief.
        Not even the soldiers watching,
        indifferent to the harrowing life
        of this woman burying her child
        in the field of a razed town
        on a morning in 1967.

    ii.

In the silence of her kneeling, there is a mountain of sorrow
smothering her bones. There are aches burning inside her body
as she stares into the small grave that contains her child.

    iii.

In another town, a man packs his child's clothes
into a box, tells him to hurry, to leave his toys behind before
they flee and hide from the soldiers approaching their town,
before the soldiers approaching their town rattle the air
with gunshots, before gunshots silence everything,
leaving everything breathless like the remains of a child
buried in the field of another razed town on a morning in 1967.

iv.

Again, it's 1967. In a room, a woman sleeps beside a man in bed.
        The man in bed is dead. The woman does not know
        that the man, her husband, is dead.

Outside, a woman combs through a field for the remains of her child.
Grief, like water, seeps through her bones. Grief, like a veil, covers her body.
Grief, like a wolf, howls inside her blood. Grief, like fog, drapes her.

v.

Each day, the children wake up to a country wriggling under the weight of war.
    They wake up to the remnants of looted villages, walls of deserted houses

pockmarked by bullets, their playgrounds littered with the bones of the dead.
    Each day, they pray for the war to end. These children, Lord.

These children, haunted by the grimness of war, stretch their hands to you
    while they are dying. I mean, they are dying while reaching out to you.

So, I begin with these children unnamed in death. I begin in the fields where
    they are buried. Forgotten. I name them in silence. In songs. In prayers.

I name them while I am awake and in my dreams. In my dreams, the children
    are gone. In my dreams, my country is burning. I name my country an abyss.

I name it a song sung in the dark of decades of unrest.

vi.

   Today, it's 2011. The children are awake again to the scent of death in the air,
to explosions in villages, in schools whose classrooms will never open to them

again like the tender arms of their dead parents. The children witness their villages
burn into shards. They know there are makeshift graves each time their beloveds

are erased by bombs. Lord, on this earth, I know that the remains
of my beloveds decay beneath the soil. I name my dead in the language

of remembrance. I plant flowers where there is emptiness.

vii.

Each day, I wake up to a country turned into a ghost house.
I watch the birds ache for a blissful world. Sometimes, they migrate

and return to witness the rubble of history. In the language of loss, my country's
name echoes louder than prayers. My country's name a knife peeling my tongue.

My country a gallows. A book of casualties. How do I breathe when the air
of my country reeks of war? My eyes singe from the smoke ascending the air.

viii.

Trees do not grow where there is rubble —

    I know this because even now in a village
        there is a man sifting through the wreckage

for the photograph of his child. He lifts what looks like a hand.
No one knows if it's a child's hand, or the hand of a man lifting

a cup of tea to his mouth before a missile shatters his window.
The man pauses. He knows the weight of the hand of history reaching from the dark:

the many dead in Mozogo town, the blood of those shot in their sleep
in Bama. The ashes of bodies years after the blasts.

The man thinks about the enormous shock in the eyes of those who stared
at the charred remains of their dead, and the fact that today the hand of history

still reaches from the dark room of forgetfulness.

ix.

Flowers do not grow where there is rubble, a woman in Kofa says, when asked
about the future of the razed villages. In my room, I measure what remains

of my love for this country where the children at the refugee camps
stay awake as hunger wrenches their bones, their mothers sobbing in the dark.

Lord, there are days I weep for them. I know they can't see me,
    but I want the birds of my mourning to reach them.

AFTER THE BLASTS

> *At least 13 people including children died when a suicide bomber blew herself up in a crowd that was fleeing an armed attack in northern Cameroon on Friday, a U.N. security report said.* — Reuters, Jan. 9th, 2021

i.

There are no songbirds in the air of a blasted country.
        There are no houses without obituaries on the walls.

In a room, there is a woman gathering the toys of her dead child.
        There is a child observing his mother's remains in bed.

Lord, where are the children who were playing in a field
        when the first bomb landed in this town?

Where is the field where the dead old woman
        left unburied beside a mosque used to walk

on evenings before the blasts?
        Where are the children rescued from half-burnt

buildings, and what happens to a child of no country,
        a child that is a refugee in another country?

ii.

Where are the children carried out of half-burnt
        buildings, and what happens to a child of no country,

a child that is a refugee in another country? At a cemetery, a woman
        places her palms on the small grave of her child

as if to bless the grave, to say, *bless you,*
        my little one buried by bombs.
          Bless you, my child.

The child's grave—
        unmarked, but still visible to his mother.

Lord, how unbearable the sadness of a mother who will spend
    the rest of her life returning to the grave of her child

to grieve her loss, to say, *bless you, my little one.*

iii.

What grief awaits the exiled, the women
    who flee home when home burns
        like coals beneath their feet?

In a letter home, a man asks those who remain
if there is anything he can do to help them.

He writes, *please, let me know what to do to help.*
I know nothing remains of the houses, the markets,
    the farmlands, the goats and fowls.

Tell me, dear ones, how can I quench the fire
      of your sorrow?

The man, a refugee, longs for home.
    The man, a refugee, knows that home is a flag

of blood planted beside the makeshift grave of a child.

THE WEIGHT OF LEAVING

for Dikwa, Gumna Kayeya, Ilewaya, Keza,
Mulfe Balalam, Mafa, and Marte

    i.

On the doors of rooms in these villages
    there are farewell notes left by families
        crossing the sea to another land.

There are unread letters on tables in rooms
        where dust inherits the belongings
            of those who will never return

to sleep in their beds, to wake up to
            the music of the wind from the fields.

    ii.

On the wall, there is a calendar detailing
    the dates of blasts, shootings, curfews;
        dates of burying and grieving the remains
of those murdered on farmlands, in the streets,
    in a mosque after prayer,
        in their cars, at the markets,
            in schools, everywhere.

    iii.

They carry with them boxes of grief   There is a language heavy with
    and jars of sorrow.   the alphabet of mourning on their lips.

They carry with them the last words   The dark thread of sorrow
    of their dead beloveds.   stretches in their eyes.

They carry with them the fragments of fractured things,   There are losses piling
    cups of tears and bowls of blood.   like sand dunes in their lives.

They carry with them the memories of years   filled with the wails of those
    on their knees, shot and left to drown   in the sea of blood.

They carry with them the smell of fields of carcasses   and gardens of unburied bones.
They carry with them the history of ruins   and the sad stories of those

               whose lives are wrecked beyond redemption.

    iv.

No one among them knows
       what awaits them in another land.

               They do not know if there are army tanks
                    in the streets.

They do not know if there is a sanctuary,
      because in their homeland
          there is nowhere safe enough for the children

to live without being martyred.

    v.

At the border of another country,
    they stand all day, the hunger in their eyes

the longing for the green of a new land.
    At dusk, they sleep in the cold,

the children uncovered.
   They do not want to return to their

coffined country, to rooms of mourning
   and streets of funerals. They do not want

to return to where birds fall into the arms of death,
   where blood saturates the earth.

               So they wait at the border, in the cold, undeterred.
               The women sing a lullaby for their dying infants.

The men search for food, beg God to send relief,
    mercy, a safe way to reach their imagined promised land.

They wait — fathers, mothers, children — all of them
    carrying boxes of grief and jars of sorrow,

        all of them searching for a home elsewhere.

WHAT THEY REMEMBER

Bakassi IDP camp, Maiduguri, Nigeria

      i.

In the forlorn hours of each night,
    the women remember their husbands

blindfolded before they are taken
    to somewhere unknown. They remember the deserted streets,

huts reduced to tombs, birds trapped in the clouds of bullets.
    Sometimes, they light candles to see the photographs

of their dead on the walls. They know there are graves
    of children left uncovered, burial grounds displaced by flood,

fields of mutilated bodies. They know there are no stars
    adorning the sky, and no one can predict when the stars

will come, when birds, absent from their nests, will return.
    Sometimes, the women sing for their children.

They promise them a basket of fruits, boxes of their favorite dolls,
    clothes for Christmas. They promise them toy cars,

toy guns, slates, balloons, paper kites,
    sandals to wear to the streets.

They promise them an eternity of bliss, but they know
    there is nothing that resembles bliss in a burning world,

in villages where bombs announce the *adhan,* where mothers
    back their children and race across the streets of smoke.

      ii.

Even at dawn, the sky wears the cloak of dusk,
    a woman, whose name is Hauwa, says.

Beside her, her child is asleep.
                Sometimes, she stands in the dark, her whole life

unfolding into aches. Into silence. Into the memory of her husband
                dragged through the rubble-strewn streets of their village.

She remembers her husband's open eyes
                in death, his body drenched in blood, his body a testament of loss.

      iii.

What is history when the dead are not remembered?
                Another woman, whose husband's corpse is still missing,

says as she paces her room. Her body a vessel of grief.
                Her life a ship sinking. In silence, she mourns.

She mourns her husband. She mourns her village. She remembers the last time
                her husband kissed her, the last time she cooked for him,

rubbed his aching back. *God, why have you forsaken me?* She asks.
                In her question, the questions of all our dead,

those whose footprints are wiped on this earth bereft of monuments for the dead.
                In her silence, the sorrow of women who grieve

with their children every night, their lives ungathered, their dreams
                buried like the hope of a country where every window

opens into a cemetery. *God, why have you forsaken me?* She repeats.
                On the table, the candlelight dies.

      iv.

On the table, the candlelight dies.
                In sleep, the children remember their homeland.

They yearn for birds in flight, for the musk of flowers and olive trees.
                They dream of a new playground, schools without bombs

planted on the walls. They reach for the sky. In their sleep, they pray to God.
                They ask God to build a country where they will be able

to sleep without bullets parting the air.
                They beg God to return their dead fathers,

to heal the wounds tended by their mothers in the stillness of these rooms
                where home is a phantom scaring them each night.

In sleep, the children remember fleeing to borders with their mothers.
                In sleep, they pant. They speak in the language of grief.

        v.

In the language of grief, the history of a country is written.
                The women know where the language aches,

where the history bears names of the dead.

Some mornings, they queue for food with their children. They wait for relief materials.
                They remember years before their villages were invaded—

How they would wake up, carry their children, and walk to their farms.
                They remember how they would cook, gather the children

and feed them from the crops they planted. They remember the cornfields,
                the orange trees climbed by their children, the hills and mountains

and brooks. They remember the laughter in the air,
                the voices of those returning home from their farms.

They remember their cattle grazing the fields, the wind swirling in the streets,
                dogs barking at night, stars roaming the sky.

They remember the moonlight stories, the children gathering at their feet,
                the night closing like a door, all of them dreaming without the dread

of being attacked. They remember the sea unstained with blood,
                fields without graves, birds singing in the evening of each day,

cocks crowing at dawn. They remember the pots of water awaiting travellers
                to fetch from them, the beds left for those who crave sleep,

the mats shared by the children. They remember everything until nothing remains
                to be remembered.

GHAZAL: MOON

        i.

Tonight, silence reigns in rooms where the children watch
    the candle lights burn to wax, knowing that there is no moon

in the sky. Sometimes, their mothers shut the windows,
    tell them to sleep because they know there will be no moon

in the sky of a country burying its children, a country where
    the children play in the streets before vanishing like the moon

during war. In treetops, there are no birds to dart,
    to delight the children who know there will be no moon

in the sky of their homeland because there will be a shooting before dawn,
    sirens of ambulances keeping them awake even when there is no moon

to see the streets congested with the wounded, with those begging
    to be taken to hospitals, those who know there will be no moon

in the sky no matter how long they pray and fast.

        ii.

In the dark, Amina holds the hand of her child as they scout
    for a place to sleep till dawn. In this land, night begins without the moon,

but with trepidation in the eyes of women praying against
    the insurgents, hoping that someday there will be moon

in the sky and there will be no insurgents ransacking their houses,
    and there will be no terror of war to bury even the light of the moon

and there will be no suffering of being in a homeland
    where no one knows when the war will end, when the moon

will return to the sky like migratory birds, like birds who flee
    the sky of a country where rockets replace the moon

on nights heavy with the cries of people herded through
 the dark to the gallows, to a place where there is no moon

for them to see the faces of those who mask their faces in the dark
   before spilling their blood under the sky of a country deserted by moon.

        iii.

Somewhere in this land, there are no children   to gaze at the sky
because the sky is a home of bullets   on nights without moon.

In her room, Balqees watches the dread   in her child's eyes before
he surrenders to sleep. She knows there is fear   in the air on nights without moon,

nights when fear drives through their bodies   the way bullets drive through their bodies
in this land where there is no cenotaph   for those who will no longer see the moon.

DARAK

         i.

In a room, Asma traces the body of her son in bed
         the way she traces the scars
                  that darken her body.

It is night in their village.
         Outside, the branches of trees
                  fall like men on the battlefield.

There is a sound rising into the air
         like the voices of those about to be slaughtered.

A sound that carries with it the cries
         of women buried beneath the bloodied
                  soil of this land.

Somewhere, a woman
         placates her child to sleep,
   says *tomorrow*
         you will wake up to a sky of stars.

         ii.

In a room, Abdullah teaches his son
         how to outpace bullets whenever
                  he goes to the streets.

There is silence engulfing the air in rooms
         abandoned by those who stay awake

tonight in a refugee camp.

         iii.

   There is a man nursing
         a woman in a room filled
         with the dread of war.
The woman is dying, like her land.
      The woman knows

              the etymology of grief,
the origin of sorrow that silences
                        her as she stares into the air.

In the sky there are clouds revealing
      the gloom that veils the days ahead.

                    There are no birds to sing
of the dead, for those who shovel

the earth tonight to bury the remains of their loved ones.

      iv.

There is a door opening in the dark.
The hand that opens the door

is the hand that reaches for mercy.
The hand that resembles the hand

of a woman scraping the earth,
exhuming from the soil the remains of her child.

      v.

            Here in Darak,
    a child watches a building become debris.

His eyes flinch.
His eyes the color of the sky
on nights of siege.

Tonight, the streets are bereft of feet.
There is silence piercing like a knife,

a knife glistening with the wetness of a child's blood.
    It is a night of siege, a woman says

to her child as she blankets her in bed.

II.

The sea is history.
　　　　—Derek Walcott

You'll die at sea.
Your head rocked by the roaring waves,
your body swaying in the water,
like a perforated boat.
　　　— Abdel Wahab Yousif

WHAT CROSSES THE SEA

A woman and two children drowned in the Rio Grande
on Friday night in Eagle Pass, Texas, after U.S. border agents
were prevented from responding, federal officials said Saturday.
      — Dennis Romero, NBC News, Jan. 13th, 2024

     i.

Not a skein of geese migrating in the sky
this morning in a country where the children
are in their rooms playing with their dolls,

their lives unscathed, their voices unmuffled,
their laughter sounding like water on days
when there are no boats loaded with migrants
     drowning at sea.

     ii.

Not the kites thrown into the sky by children
who play in fields where there are no bomb craters,
     where there are no bullets
          trailing their tender bodies.

     iii.

Lord, what crosses the sea are babies wrapped in shawls,
    placed inside cots by mothers fleeing
        on nights when soldiers raid houses
          and leave everything dead.

     iv.

Somewhere today, there are remains of children unrecognized by their mothers,
        by those who bend their backs
          to see these remains, to know
            what terror looks like.

     v.

What crosses the sea are the children of refugees.
    Like the sky, the sea is not a home for children.

In the Rio Grande River, the drowned bodies of a woman and her two children
    are washed ashore. They look like waste, like discarded items.

Lord, what's home when there are families collecting the bones of their dead
    inside plastic bags? In my homeland, there are men

searching the debris for the bones of their children,
    for the toys of their children, for the shoes of their children.

In the streets, there are bodies displayed like the photographs
    of missing children. What's home when the hands of children

reach for the still hands of their drowned fathers, for the open arms
    of their dead mothers? Tonight, I pray for the women

backing their children as they cross the sea. I pray for the waterlogged remains
    of children beneath the immeasurable body of the sea.

I pray for the mothers waiting all night at sea for the return
    of boats carrying the corpses of their children.

I pray for those who clasp their palms, who lift their clasped palms
    into the sky to ask God for mercy as their boats capsize,

        as their last cries permeate the air.

REQUIEM AT SEA I

AFA

The sea is very funny, papa. But it not making me laugh. Some say this sea is dead fisherman laughing. Some say is noise of all the fisherman woman crying. Sea in Dauphin never quiet. Always noise, noise.
— Derek Walcott's *The Sea at Dauphin*

i.

The boats abandoned at the edge of the sea
    belong to dead fishermen. The cries ruffling the air
        each night belong to the drowned bodies

of migrants, to those who are nameless in death,
    whose bodies are testaments
        to the sea's long history of drowning.

Some days, the hands of the sea rise and fall
    like the hands of mothers carrying their babies
        on rubber boats before the sea turns against their dream

of reaching their promised land. Lord, what remains of those
    who will never return home to embrace their children,
        those whose eyes will never see the sky

laden with stars? What remains of the boats without
    the men sailing them? In the dark book of history,
        the sea contains the bodies of men freighted
            through its passage during slavery.

ii.

From Africa, my ancestors are crammed
on slave ships, and ferried across
the Mediterranean.

They arrive in Jamestown in 1619.

On cotton plantations, they bend their backs
and sing slave songs.

They water the fields with tears and blood.
        They remember those drowned at sea.

They remember the slave ships as coffins.
        They ache for homeland.

Even till now, they ache for homeland.

    iii.

In 1803, 75 Igbo slaves are stacked
on a vessel named *York,* on a vessel
    that ferries them to Dunbar Creek,
    where their cries traverse the world,
    where they rise, like a tide,
against their captors; where they sing
their songs of victory and march into the sea,
their bodies merging with water,
their bodies dissolving into songs.

    iv.

Tonight, there are women gazing
    at the sinister sky, women grieving men

drowned at sea, women carrying the cross of loss
    as they stand in the darkness that remains

of their lives, as they remember the sea— a mass grave
    for those who, like Afa, search for their daily bread;

a chart of losses for those who seek it,
    their fingers touching its liquid edges, its fragile body,

its carnivorous mouth swallowing the dreams of beloveds
    fleeing their homelands to foreign countries.

ELEGY FOR THE DROWNED

        i.

On the vast body of water
    there are waves heavy
      with the final prayers of the drowned.

There is a catalogue of losses,
    a depository of last words spoken
      by those whose bloated bodies
        will never be retrieved from the sea.

God, beneath the sea are pieces of bones
    that belong to fathers who once shouldered
      their children in the light of the world,
        mothers whose voices once tended
          their infants with lullabies.

    ii.

How do we measure the depth of water
    that claims our loved ones?

How do we track the footprints
    of the drowned on water?

In the register of drowned bodies,
    there are names of forgotten children:

Mahmud, Abdullah, Zubair, Hashem,
Uthman, Kabir, Hakeem, Hassan,
    Alan, Khadijah, Hassanah,
      Zeenat, Ahmad

all of them children, too many to be counted.
    All of them children who will not wake up

again to the sky laden with stars,
    to the smell of grass, to the butterflies in the fields,

to grandmothers' stories in rooms where there are lanterns
                                  on the tables, joy in the voices

    of grandfathers narrating the stories of animals.
They are children whose remains are buried

    at sea, children who will not hear again
                the muezzin's call to prayer, children who will

never return to attend schools, to help their grandmothers
        fetch water, to feed goats, to plant flowers,

and sleep on mats outside their huts at night
                while the breeze blows past.

        iii.

Tonight, there are women holding a vigil
        on behalf of all their drowned loved ones.

There are mothers cradling the photographs of their drowned children,
          fathers performing the ritual of mourning their drowned children.

They weep for the sea and the remains of the beloveds beneath it.
        They weep for the sea and the blood of the drowned flowing through it.

They weep for the dreams perished at sea; dreams dismantled by the tide of water.
        They ache for what's gone, like their drowned beloveds.

DOORS

        i.

The truth is there are no doors
        that will not close at the end of life.

In death, I watched the door
        of my grandfather's body close,

unopen to the light escaping into the hospital ward
        through the open windows.

At his funeral, I opened the door of his casket
        to touch his hands and say my last prayers

before his remains were eased into the earth.
        Lord, how quiet the door of hope on days

when our beloveds cross the borders of the world
        to the afterlife.

        ii.

There are *doors of no return* bearing the weight of slavery
        on Gorée Island. In Ouidah.

There are doors leading us to rooms where the cries of the enslaved
        unfurl into memories of the middle passage:

ancestors stowed on slave ships to the new world.
        In the silence of history, the horse of remembrance

races through forgotten fields of graves belonging to anonymous dead.
        Lord, how weighty the doors of grief opening into decades

of unrecorded deaths of the enslaved.

iii.

Lord, I wait at the door of your mercy
      on nights heavy with the sorrow of remembering the dead.

I know there is no door that will lead to you
      but this door of prayers. On this earth, my dead are scattered

across the fields and there are no names on their headstones.
      My dead are drowned bodies of migrants crossing the sea to Europe,

the wrecks of their boats on water. My dead are children clinging
      to their mothers that are clinging to the delicate rope of hope

      as their boats begin to sink into the Mediterranean Sea.

iv.

There is a door of mourning opening into the room of my life
      after my grandfather's death.

There is a door that leads to fields where children are interred
      and where their mothers stand in the cold of each day

to mourn, to lay wreaths on their graves.
      There is a map of sorrow unfolding into a door

that will guide us to burial grounds strewn with remains
      of the forgotten enslaved.

How weighty the history of slavery, Lord. How brutal the memories
      we carry with us. Today, there is a door of despair opening inside me

that needs to be closed. There is a door that will lead us to the sea,
      that will ferry us across the borders of the world

      to the afterlife.

REQUIEM AT SEA II

       i.

On a boat off the Island of El Hierro,
    there is a child clutching his mother's arm
        as their boat drowns.

    In the sky, there are birds singing
        a requiem for those whose bodies,
           in death, bear the horror of water.

Some days, the sea offers its gift of death
    to those who flee to it,
        those who beg to be transported
           across it to a chimeric El Dorado.

    ii.

At sea, there are boats departing each night
        with migrants aboard:

mothers fleeing war-torn homelands,
    fathers carrying bags of items

salvaged from bombed buildings, the children quiet
    in their mothers' arms, their whole lives marked

by the tragedy of searching for a phantom paradise.
    The fishermen, their lives bound to the ritual of fishing

and waiting for the submerged bodies of migrants to return to the shore,
    wait night after night to bury those who are unlucky

to cross the ominous passage of the sea. They know that nothing
    is safe in the fragile arms of water.

    iii.

Near Bodrum, the body of a three-year-old
    Alan Kurdi lies face down on the beach.

On the news, his name reaches the world, which wonders
        how tragic the death of a child at sea.

Lord, there is no statistician to calculate the number
        of drowned migrants, those whose bodies

are unfound years after waters turned their boats
        into wrecks, into losses mourned by those who stay awake

each night, stunned by how nothing survives the sea,
        how year after year there are boats carrying

families fleeing homelands during war
                to the other side of the sea.

HUNGER

i.

In the vocabulary of water, there is a word, *hunger*.
There is a *boat*. There is an empty boat on water.

> Sometimes, there is *hunger* and there is a *boat*
> full of *migrants*. There is no asylum in the dark

body of water, in the way the sea carries
the omen of tragedy. There is hunger

> in the howl of the sea, starvation in the way
> the boat-strewn sea quakes.

Today, there are fishermen singing a funeral song
for drowned lives. Their canoes are empty,

> like their hope.

ii.

In the vocabulary of water, there is grief.
There is grief as weighty as a *boat* and *hunger*.

No one knows how to quell the hunger of the sea.
How to bind the tongue of the sea, how to say,

this is enough. Tonight the sea will stay awake again
while another *boat* of migrants

will begin to voyage. At the edge of the sea,
the bodies of the drowned will be still.

> Among them a woman and her child.
> Among them a man and his wife.

There will be no one to sing a threnody
for the dead. The door of the sea

will be closed. In its room,
        the remains of our dead.

In the diary of water, there are no names
        enough for every drowned body.

        iii.

In the vocabulary of water, there is a word called
hunger. Meaning the sea opening

        its wide mouth to drown our loved ones.

Meaning voyaging
        across the sea on days
                when the sea rages,

on nights heavy with the cries
        of the drowned, of those waiting
to be rescued from the talons of the sea.

THE GRIEF THAT STARTLES THE WATERS

does not have a name.
    Like the remains of the dead after every war.

Sometimes, it appears that there are innumerable bodies
        settling, like sediment, on the sea floor.

    Think of the names buried in the quietude
        of an evening,
the fishermen returning home with empty nets.

      Imagine us packed on a boat,
        our bodies aching
            the way a caged bird aches for flight.

On the news, there are migrants
    whose bodies are unknown

because the sea does not offer a tag
        to those who embrace it
            and its rite of drowning.

Sometimes, I call it loss.
          That the night will come

to us with an unmarked mass grave
        for our dead. That water, as simple

as it sounds on our tongues,
        is an archive of grief,

a place where history begins with those whose memories,
    today, still grip our hearts as more news of drowning

        reaches us whose lives are cradled in despair,
        us whose names will dissolve

          in the water of forgetfulness
            when the boat of death arrives
            to ferry us to the end of the world.

III.

I'm too late,
again, another space emptied by loss.
— Natasha Tretheway

MERCY

1.

There is a wolf howling in this grief. There is a wall collapsing into this sorrow. Today, I kneel in a field of graves. I touch where the aches clench my bones, where nothing can soothe the pang of my wounds. I map my wounds to know where my father's name brightens and dims, where weeds claim his mother's grave. I wake up and my dead are still dead. I reach out to them through my wounds that burn each time I recite their names.

2.

I stand in the dark of grief. In the desolation of years pledged to mourning my dead. I know where the wounds simmer, where the wounds groan and quiet. I pray for your mercy, Lord. I know the weight of mourning. Somewhere, there is a man folding the clothes of his dead wife. There is a man writhing in grief, searching for ways to forget the wounds that remain unforgettable no matter the number of years spent tending them.

3.

I pine for the flight of birds. For their music defying the unfading chorus of grief.
I ache to be like the birds. I want my arms to be light, unburdened by the weight of wounds.
I want my knees to be light, spared by years of kneeling on the cold floor of my room.
I want a song that begins and ends without the wounds burning, without my hope crumbling, without the room of my heart becoming a morgue for my dead.

4.

I stand in the despair of a dying world. I stand in the silence of a world where there is no solace in mourning. No respite in longing for the dead. Today, I find no comfort in kneeling in a field of graves. Watching the wind hurtle across the vast acres of burial grounds. Lord, I crave your mercy in the hours of mourning. I crave your mercy on nights when the wounds wrench my heart.

5.

I watch the birds return each day to their nests. I do not know the number of years they will spend before succumbing to death. But I know, Lord, that the birds, like me, will surrender to death someday in this world, where we must stand in the desolation of years in the absence of our beloveds.

THE ORIGIN OF WOUNDS

        i.

I begin in a hospital ward where my mother stares
      at the still body of her father in astonishment,

where she watches, slowly, the grief gathering in her eyes
      as she touches her father's cold body,

as she kneels beside his corpse, her mouth quivering each time
      she attempts to speak. I begin where his absence

unspools into tears, where silence thickens in his room on mornings
      bereft of him waking up to listen to the radio,

to watch through the window the trees outside his room,
      the birds in flight, the wind whirling in the streets.

I begin where my mother weeps, where her body surrenders
      to the agony of knowing that her father will never return

to his room, to his table to read the letters from his beloveds.

        ii.

I begin where death enters a room and meets a beloved
      gasping for breath.

I begin with the solemn voices of the bereaved in rooms
      where their beloveds surrender to death.

    I begin where nothing exists, where the wounds widen
          in the hearts of the bereaved.

        iii.

Lord, I know there is the certainty of the end
      each time I hear the funeral hymns

reaching me from a burial ground.

      I know sometimes there are loved ones
    remembering their dead beloveds in the quietude of rooms

        where darkness invades everywhere.

    iv.

I begin in my mother's room
    where nothing resembles joy,

       where the photographs of her dead
          drape the walls,

where some nights she counts the rosary beads
        as she prays for her dead.

    v.

    I begin where the wounds begin with silence,
        and then prayers,

and then silence. I begin with silence the weight of a body
        in death, the weight of a casket containing

the corpse of a beloved.
      I begin where the bereaved depart for their homes,

where they turn to leave, the dead lonely in their graves,
        the dead unaware of the bereaved departing

      for their homes.

    vi.

I end where there is no healing for us
    who wake up each day to tend
        the wound of mourning our dead.

GOD

               i.

Here is my wound the shape
      of my grandmother's face in death.

Here is my grandmother's body
      pressed beneath the soil,

beneath the heavy clods of earth
      where all things decompose,

where the light of the world
      can no longer reach the dead.

Here are the dark soles of loss.
      In the vast fields of the world,

the dead are quiet like my hands
      aching to touch them.

Here are my grandmother's dust-laden
      photographs inside a box.

Here are the gowns of mourning,
      the handkerchiefs of tears,

the black berets of funerals, the sad shoes
      worn by the bereaved.

Sometimes, I imagine the fields without
      the bodies, God. I think about the ancestors

buried here before my birth. Some days,
      I look through the window

at the flowers sprouting where
      there are bodies whose names

I do not know. How empty the body
        of a beloved in death, and how weighty

the earth that covers it. Here, beneath this dirt,
        is my grandmother's body, God.

Here are her belongings in a room where
        dust settles on them, where nothing reminds

me of hope. I know, too, that nothing can stir
        the dead from their graves,

from this earth where everything
                is fated to putrefy.

        ii.

Here is the comb stuffed with the strands
        of my grandmother's gray hair.

Here is the last dress she wore,
        the last medication she took.

Here is the sky opening into wounds,
        the earth burying the dead.

Here are my grandmother's eyes that will
        never open again to see the sparrows

in the sky. Here are the trees of sorrow, the trees
of mourning lowering their branches in the wake
        of my grandmother's death.

Here are the rigid roots of grief,
        the stunted twigs of hope,

the shriveled flowers of dreams.
        Here is the body's last dance.

I mean, my grandmother's last dance
        before the stroke tethered her to bed.

ALL AROUND ME

There is a field of grief. There is a man standing in a field
    of graves. There is a man who bears my father's face standing

before a grave that is his mother's grave. There is a man standing,
    holding a bouquet of funeral flowers, holding a bouquet of funeral flowers

to be placed on the grave of his mother. In this field, there is nothing lush.
    There is nothing delightful about a field of graves.

In this field of graves, there is a woman approaching a man standing
    before his mother's grave. The woman is my mother joining

my father in this performance of grief. I do not say they are dancing.
    I do not say they are singing. I mean, my parents stand

in a field of graves. They stand before the grave of my father's mother.
    They know there is nothing that can bloom in this field.

There is neither a piano nor a guitar to be played in this grief.
    All the trees are quiet. All the trees are quiet

like the dead. In this grief, there are decades of graves. There are decades
    of silence, years of remembrance and forgetfulness. There are traces

of dead trees, remains of abandoned graves. There are neither camels
    nor donkeys visiting these graves. Lord, how quiet a field of graves.

How endless the ritual of mourning, the performance of grief in a field of graves
    where my parents stand this morning to place a bouquet of flowers

on the grave of my grandmother.

IN PRAISE OF THE END

                i.

There is no number of years that will be enough
    to dress the wounds of a mother. There is no number of years

that will be enough to dress the wounds of a mother
    mourning her father. There is no number of years that will be enough

to dress the wounds of a mother mourning her father in a room where all the things
    that exist bear the burden of his absence. There is no number of years

that will be enough to dress the wounds of a mother mourning her father in a room
    where all the things that exist reek of the father's absence:

the clothes left unfolded in bed, the family album inside a drawer,
    the radio on the table, the letters left unopened on the table, the air bereft

of his voice as another day arrives without him listening to morning news
    on the radio, watching through the windows the flowers and their assembly

of colors, the trees and their branches, a shield for the birds.

                ii.

There is no way to fill the hollow in the heart of a mother
    grieving her departed father. There is no way to fill the hollow

in the heart of a mother grieving her departed father in this world where my mother,
    who has buried her father, knows the many ways that grief can enter

the body and ruin it. There is no damage to be done to the body other than
    the damage done by grief. In my mother's grief, there is her father dying,

dead and buried. There is no plot of land without the remains of a father.
    In the fields of the world, my mother's father's grave is bereft of headstones .

In the fields of the world, there are graves without names. There are graves
    of children, of women whose hands once lifted their babies into the air

of the world. There are fathers whose lives are unsung in death,
                whose graves are marked in dirt.

        iii.

The end returns to us the way a boat returns to the shore.
    The way the bees return to their hives.

In the diary of death, there are names of beloveds whose rooms
    are empty of joy. There are names of beloveds whose remains

are not buried at home. Lord, the end returns bearing the sorrow of departure,
    of standing at the funeral of a beloved to sing the hymns of sorrow,

the monody of loss, the melancholic song of those who witness
      the return of the body to dust.

ELEGY I

i.

More than once, I have prayed for the Eden of healing in a room
      where I can't reach my dead, where I can't hear them laugh

or pronounce my name again in this world where nothing will survive us.
      Some nights, I watch the gale of grief strip me of the hope of listening

to my grandfather's voice the way I did before the door of his heart
      shut in the hospital bed. Lord, I have longed for the presence of what's

buried beneath dirt. Today, all the wounds of my heart bear the names
      of my dead. Outside my room, there are leaves rotting.

There are bats hanging their heads forlornly. I do not know the antidote
      to what's breathless like the dead, like these hours of recollecting

           what will never return.

ii.

There is no Eden in the pain throbbing the body before death.
      In bed, my grandmother spent years watching the bricks of her body

fall, each one of the fallen bricks a wound that rendered me weary
      of this world and the trauma that we must carry through each day

of reaching for the Eden on earth, for a door to open into a room
      where the beloveds do not mourn.

iii.

There is a sadness looming in my chest, opening the small room of my heart
      each time I long for my dead. There are clouds congregating in the sky of my life.

More than once, I have prayed for the eternity of life. I know where the knife
      of sorrow parts my bones, where the garden of my hope does not bloom.

Lord, how can I walk when the ground is slippery with tears,
      when the earth contains the remains of my beloveds?

iv.

There is no haven in the body mourning the dead. On nights
   of mourning, I watch the light of my body flicker

in a room where I can't hear the voices of my beloveds.
    How unbearable the work of mourning, Lord. The living wake up

each day to the news of a beloved's passing. In this world, none of us
   will be spared by death when the bell tolls, when our bodies become

impossible to be revived and returned to the world of the living.

BLESSED BE THE BODY IN DEATH

i.
and blessed be the hands touching
 the body in death to know the coldness
 of the body.

Blessed be the hands dressing the body in death,
 carrying the body in death,

folding the bed sheets that reek of the body
 before death and in death.

Blessed be the stillness of the body in death,
 the stench of the body that shows how quick

the body decays in death and how sad that the body,
 before death, never understands the ordinariness
 at the end of life.

Blessed be my grandmother's body that,
 in death, was carried tenderly from her bed to the casket

and to the grave.

ii.
Blessed be her body wrapped
 in a burial shroud,

prayed on by the bereaved who bowed
 to Allah as they prepared the body for the earth.

Blessed be the last days of her life:
 the stroke deepening, ravaging her to silence,

to the futility of healing.

Blessed be the silence of her mouth
 and the shut doors of her eyes in death.

Blessed be the horse of grief
            trampling the bodies of the bereaved,

the birds screeching in the sky on the day of her passing,
            the sky clouded and heavy with sorrow.

ELEGY II

                    i.

At dusk, a caravan of birds
      voyages homeward while the world sleeps.

Sometimes, I wonder how the birds travel across
      the sky without a map, how they perch on trees

and desert their nests during a storm. In this world,
      there are days when we pray for the miracle

of survival, to leave our rooms and return without
      bullets lodged in our bones, to hear the voices

of our beloveds without sorrow muffling them.
      But there are days, too, when we wake up

to the ungraspable sorrow of burying a loved one,
      to the emptiness of a beloved's room,

to the withering of flowers in a garden doubling
      as the unmarked grave of a woman.

                    ii.

Lord, we know we will know loss the way the birds
      know their ways of survival in the sky

in this world where the bereaved know the weight
      of silence at the funeral ground.

We know nothing will heal the wounds we carry from
      one day to another, the wounds that bear the places

covered in ruins. In the transient years of our lives
      we will wake up some days to know despair,

to drag our feet across places emptied by loss.
      We will bury our loved ones without adorning

their graves with flowers. How brief the joy
        of being alive, Lord.

How unsteady the light of hope we carry like an urn
        as we continue to wander,

as we spend each day longing for the days ahead,
        for years that might not meet us alive

in this world where each day
        there is the stillness of the dead,

the stillness of everything that reeks
        of the eternity of our loved ones' absence.

MONTHS AFTER MY GRANDFATHER'S DEATH

      i.

The trees outside the window of his room
      have not stopped grieving.

Each morning, their leaves litter the earth.
      Their branches bend like pallbearers

lowering the body into the ground.
      Maybe this is a ritual, or a way of saying,

see what happens to everything that remains
in the absence of a loved one.

See how the bereaved stand, each one of them
      trembling in the cold of mourning,

bewildered by the act of witnessing how the body
      returns to dust.

      ii.

During my grandfather's last days
      nothing could lift his eyes to the sky

to see the cranes migrate. In the hospital bed,
      he murmured words that sounded like prayers,

like the longing to bask in the light of hope
after days of passing through the throes of sickness.

Lord, how pale the body becomes as the light of life wanes,
      as the door of the eyes closes, as the hands stiffen.

On the day breath exited my grandfather's body,
      the earth was swarmed with leaves.

The birds' voices were filled with dirges.
      Maybe this is what it means to sorrow,

to know that the task of mourning can never be done alone.
Because somewhere today, the bereaved gather
under the tent to mourn their dead beloveds.

There are places where they are about to lower the dead into the earth.
See the dogs barking in the streets late at night,

the sky displaying their grief through the clouds.
See how, months after my grandfather's passing,

the trees outside the window
of his room never stop mourning.

GUIDE TO VISITING THE DEAD

Bring vases of flowers and your prayers.
      Walk the long rows of graves to read the names
           on the headstones.

Remember that beneath each grave
        there is a man who once planted seeds on this earth,
      a woman whose hands once touched
           something bright and colorful.

Understand this fact. That there are graves
        without headstones, graves left unweeded,
           forgotten by the relatives of the dead.

Pause. Listen to the tender songs of the birds
         returning to the trees that surround the graves.
            Stand in the wind that swirls, carrying dust

from the graves of the dead across the world.
          Locate the grave of your father or your mother
        among the long rows of graves.

Once you find it, you must kneel before it.
         Kneel because you must listen for the voice
           of your dead in the quietude of their grave.

You must cup your hands and pray for your dead
      who are alone in their graves.
          You must mourn the dead.
              Weep if you must.

On this earth the dead are legion. There are those buried
        at sea, those buried in exile, those whose
          bodies are never found
                  no matter how long we search for them.

IV.

Many corpses are stacked, Mother once told me,
because there's no space.
— Tarfia Faizullah

EMPTINESS

        i.

Not even the sound of a bell
        can wake the dead that lie still

            beneath this land.

    No one will
        wake up again to listen

to daily news,
        or walk

            the streets without thinking about

  the speed of a bullet   reaching

            for
                the heart of a child,

while his mother,

      aware of the grief awaiting her,

        screams her son's name into the dark air

of this land.

    ii.

      In a room,

        a woman cups the light of a matchstick

as she searches for the remnant of a candle.

        Her husband is dead, his body deposited

at an unknown morgue.

          During war, no one knows

where all the dead are buried.

          There are those buried where they fall,

where their hands open for the world

          to see how empty they are,

how ordinary everything becomes.

    iii.

In the stillness of grief, a woman

carries the remains of her child

        before begging another woman to help her place

her on her back.

    iv.

In this land, there is nowhere

          spacious enough to contain all the dead.

  Sometimes, the dead are exploded body parts scattered in the streets.

      In death,
          their charred remains

        remind the world of how bombs
could turn everywhere
    into a field of sorrow,

    into a field   where a man buries his child

before hanging himself.

TO RETURN TO THIS LAND

                i.

|undrowned|
                |is to not voyage across the sea|

|Today|
    |there are fishing boats|
            |marked as deadly at sea|
        |half-
        eaten bodies|
            |of fishermen|
                    afloat   on

— — — — — — — water — — — — — — — — — — — — — — — —
— —

as twilight heralds another
            |unrecorded| tragedy.

            ii.

        |In the history|
            |of the sea|
|there are bodies of families|
            |settling|
                |beneath|
    |the sea floor|

        iii.

|There are no dreams here|
        |If at all there are dreams|
            |they become flotsam|
    |shards of lives|
        |buried| |in a liquid casket|

      iv.

|In the sky|
    |a flock of birds|

|They are not like us|
　　　　　　　　|who race|
　　　　　　　　　　　　　|to the sea|
|each time|
　　　　|the earth turns into a killing ground|

|a storehouse of bullets and bombs|
　　　　　　　　　　　|for our living and dead children|

　　　　　　　v.

　　|Here|
　　　　　　|the light of joy|　　|flutters|
　　　　　　　　　　　　　　　and dies|
|each time|
|the boats|
　　　　|of drowned bodies|
　　　　　　　　　　　|return|
|to shore|

　　　　　　|Sometimes|
　　　　　　　　|there are bodies|
　　　　　　　　　　　|unfound|
　　　　|on the body of the sea|
　　　　　　　　　　　　|until months after| |until grief|
　　　　|like water|
　　　　　　　　|soaks|
|the relatives|
　　　　|of those missing|
　　　　　　　|after a shipwreck|

　　　　　　vi.

|Today|
　　　|I think|
　　　　　　|about all the migrants|
　　　　　　　　　　　|lost to the sea|
　　　　　　　　　　　　　　|to the whirlwind of loss|

|that engulfs everywhere|
           |in this land|
                      |where there are open graves|
|for our dead|

           |Lord|
                |who will sorrow over
                                these losses|
                |these dreams of lights|
|that never survive the day|?

|Beneath the sea|
           |the children of occupied countries|
                                |sons and daughters of those praying
                      to you|
|to heal the wide wounds|
                                          |of the world|
|in a mosque tonight|

           vii.

|There are no flowers for the dead|
                      |buried at sea|
|no gravestones|
|no one to write their epitaphs|
                      |no one to hold the arms of refugees|
as they drown|
           |as they reach for the world that's
                                                    |distant|

           viii.

     |What becomes of those who visit the sea each day|

|to grieve the invisible corpses|

                |of their loved ones|

                              |those who wonder how ominous|
|the body of water|?

                |There are no names|
|for seafarers lost to the sea|
|no names for those who are gone|

                |beyond the tweets of birds|

|who return to the sea daily|

                      |to grieve|

|human ruins|

DUSK, AGAIN

Dalori IDP camp, Maiduguri, Nigeria

i.

The children gaze at the sky
        but there is no moon to lighten

the burden of war in their lives.
        Their mouths heavy with unanswered prayers,

unfulfilled wishes passed
                like
                        a baton
                                on days when they pine for God's healing
for their multitude of aches.

ii.

Tonight, they crave water,

but there is no water
        because the sea is full
                      of drowned bodies
        and
the land is war-torn,   an image of loss
to those who know   how war can bury
even the last glow of a light.

    One of the children, Ahmed,
        crawls to his mother who reclines
            on a bullet-ridden wall.

        His belly, sunken by hunger;
     his life, uncertain, like the lives of children during war.

To these children, there is no paradise on this earth
        where graves replace their playground.

          iii.

In the lexicon of grief,
          every word means loss.

Each night, the children look into the dark space
  of grief to see how everything becomes ruins.

          Some days, they wake up to a country
             mourning her future.

On the faces of those who
      walk the streets,
         there is fear darker than dusk.

                    iv.

             Somewhere, a woman bathes
               the remains of her child.

        I want his body to be a proof of war,
            of my trauma, she says.

Her eyes, teary, could drown
      the earth and everything that inhabits it.

This is what remains of this land,
    of this country where each house is a tomb.

Each tree a substitute
        for a missing child.

Each stone
    a gravestone.

        Each voice
 a chorister   of dirges.

     v.

On the long list of the dead,
      there are omitted names:

Names of men slain
                in their rooms.

Names of those singing
                the anthem of their homeland

as they drown at sea.

                vi.

What else do you want to know
          about this land that hasn't been

spoken in the language of blood?
          The faces of those who remain

                are covered in blood.

                vii.

Blood tars the streets.
                Blood pours like rain, floods farmlands.

Blood inside the pails once used to fetch water.
                Blood inside bowls.

Blood in these lines.
          Blood caressing

the mouth of a soldier's gun pointed at a child
                begging to be carried to where

his mother's corpse lies.

COFFINS

In the streets of Dogon Noma,
        coffins look like paper boats to children.

They are arranged like boxes.
        Sometimes, they are shaped

like the cupped palms of women who pray
        for the return of their abducted husbands.

In silence, a man sits beside the coffin of his wife
        and offers prayers to the wind of grief that passes.

He knows the ritual of praying for the dead,
        for the drowned fishermen unreturned to their villages

for a mass burial. *To live in this place is to mourn,*
        Aisha says as she listens to news of explosions

on the radio. Some nights, the smell of blood
        clogs the noses of the villagers.

They lift candle lights into the air to see the distressed faces
        of those who knock on their doors,

who run from the arms of war to another home of war.
        Each time their children wake up, they ask

if the blasts are over. But nothing is edging to the end
        because outside there are coffins

that look like paper boats, like the boats of fishermen
        whose corpses are not returned to their villages

for a mass burial.

GHAZAL: RUINS

Who will sleep tonight in this country of ruins?
 Abdullah asks, his village filled with ruins.

In his room, there are newspapers stacked on the table.
Each one of them bears the names of those buried beneath ruins.

On the walls of empty houses, there are bullet holes.
They remind us of children buried as martyrs in this land of ruins.

Some nights, there are loved ones remembering exiled friends
and families. They know they will never return to this land of ruins.

In each room, there are mothers speaking to their children in whispers.
They know that the walls have ears, and bombs bury every light in this country of ruins.

If you are asked the meaning of home in school, a father tells
his child, tell your teacher that *home is a relic of ruins.*

If you are asked what home means after a blast, a mother says
to her child, tell them that *home is a field full of the dead and ruins.*

WHAT REMAINS

                i.

Not the horses whinnying in the fields. Not the schooners, the pigeons,
    the nightingales and their vocation of songs. Not my homeland bereft of fractures

and wounds. Not my homeland and the children in their rooms,
    unvisited by the grief of the world. Not the world without bullets.

Not the bullets without those shooting them, targeting the children
    at schools, in the streets. Not the children without wounds in their eyes,

sorrow in their words. Not the mothers without their rooms filled with candlelight
    on nights of funerals. Not funerals without some dead beloveds still missing.

Not the missing ones without their names forgotten. Not only the forgotten names
    of the missing but also their unrecognized faces. In this land, there are doors

that will never open again into rooms full of children giggling as they play on the cushions.
    There are rooms that will never again be filled with the tender voices of couples

in beds, their lives intact until bullets unlock the doors to silence them.
    In the streets, there are faces scarred by war, faces bearing the emblem of grief.

There is a woman wrapping a baby in a shawl of blood. There is a woman wrapping
    a baby in a shawl of grief. Lord, there is a woman who could be my mother,

who could be anyone in this world of unbridled sorrow.

                ii.

This morning, there is a man pruning his dead wife's garden. The man bends
    his back to water the flowers. Sometimes, in this land, there are graves

where there are supposed to be flowers. There are no flowers on unmarked graves.
    There are no flowers enough to mark all the graves. There is no cemetery expansive

enough to contain all the bodies recovered from the ruins of blasts. There is no music.
    All the birds, like all the children, ache for a sky bereft of smoke.

iii.

In a field, there are men exhuming the bones of their dead to be buried
    in another land. Sometimes, in this land, the dead do not rest in peace.

They are carried like heirlooms from one land to another. They are carried like boxes
    of old photographs, sacks of losses, diaries of names that belong to missing beloveds.

They are carried like secrets shared in the dark of night in rooms where the beloveds
    surrender to the uncertainty of their survival. They are carried like the gifts of clothes

and bracelets from a dead grandmother.

BURY US

            i.

Not in graves dug in a hurry,
            dug by hands that once held newborns,

flowers on birthdays, love letters from distant families.
            Bury us not in graves dug by hands

that once held cups of water and tea, photographs of beloveds;
            hands that once made something come alive,

hands that once tended the aching backs of beloveds.
            Bury us tenderly. Bury us separately.

We know it is difficult to do that in a land like ours:
            blood-laden acres of land, bones of the dead

scattered like confetti, shoes of dead children
            found with bullets inside them, clothes soaked in blood.

            ii.

We know that the next morning is uncertain,
            and each morning begins with a funeral mass

for those murdered in the middle of the night.
            Sometimes, it takes courage to sleep

and wake up unhurt, unblown by bombs buried
            in nearby mosques, bombs strapped

to the backs of children in the streets, bombs thrown
            like balloons into the air.

iii.

If we die tomorrow and nothing remains
        of this land, bury us in places where

our children's graves lie, where their bodies repose
              and decompose.

Bury us not in fragments. Gather our bones
        even though it is difficult

to assemble all the bones scattered on this land.
        All the bones silent, singing;

all the bones asking the difficult question of revenge.
        Can't you hear the bones wailing,

the bones turning beneath this earth, the bones
        speaking in the language of dirt?

All the bones found here and there. The bones
        held like heirlooms, like gifts of tragedy

in the light of another tragedy.

        Bury us anywhere we call home.

ODE TO LAST WISHES

                i.

I have lived long enough to know
        that sometimes a man will wake up

to weep because he has no child to hold his hand
        in a room where his body will succumb

to the throes of death. I have lived long enough
        to know the quick atrophy of the body,

the language of grief cuddling the tongues of the bereaved,
        of those who stand at the funeral of a beloved,

their lives weighty with mourning. Lord, I know the ritual
        of death, the wounds festering in the hearts

of those in rooms where they hold the photographs of their loved ones.
        I know that someday the clock of my breath will stop working

but Lord, please, I don't want to die in a foreign land.

                ii.

At the end of my life, I want to die in the presence
        of my beloveds in a room that smells of my body

and the bodies of all those I have loved.
        I want to die in my country of birth, my remains buried

in that soil that covers my ancestors and where there are hills
        and mountains that I climbed as a child.

I want to listen to the wild songs of the world
        before I close my eyes and I want to bask in the full light

of the moon and watch the wind gather dust in its arms.
        I want to die in a land where my umbilical cord

is buried and I want my grave marked
        and I want to depart in the way of my ancestors

whose bodies lie beneath this earth where
        all of us will return to at the end of life.

IN PRAISE OF THE WORLD

                      i.

Praise the horse of remembrance
        standing this morning in a desolate field

of graves and praise my endless longing for the dead.
        Praise the dead. Praise the veil of silence

that shrouds the remains of our beloveds beneath this earth
        that will outlive us. Praise this earth again

and praise the ants reducing the dead to bones, to what archeologists
        will return to centuries later to see what becomes

of us buried beneath this earth where everything decays.
        Praise each day that meets us inhaling the good air

of the world, the birds lifting their wings in praise of flight.
        Praise the flight of birds and their quest for survival.

Praise survival. Praise our courage to carry the aches
        of the world through days of mourning.

Praise the trees and their long arms and their rigid roots
        and praise the root of all things that lead us here:

the ancestors guiding our steps, gifting us the light of wisdom
        to see through the passage of time to the end

of the world. Praise the ancestors for carrying us through
        the storm of the world, for their rituals

and chants and poetry in a world where joy is fickle and sorrow
        is a cart arriving each day at our doorsteps,

waiting for us to open our doors.
    Praise tribal traditions and praise my mother's stories

and her voice reaching me across the borders of the world
    and praise the world and the flowers growing and the animals

grazing the vast fields of the world.

    ii.

Praise the fragile arms of hope. Praise the coffins built for us

who will someday surrender to death in rooms and hospital wards
    where we will not be able to listen to the birds sing

and watch the trees sway their long hands as our breaths exit this world.
    Praise this world. Praise the tender touches of friends

and strangers that we carry with us through each day of encounters.

Praise the futility of everything in death: our quest for survival,
    our hunger for fame, our laurels, the largeness of our dreams

that sometimes keep us awake as we map the future even when we are not certain
    that the future will meet us alive in this world

where in death our palms will be empty, our bodies dressed in burial clothes,
    lowered into this earth where ants will reduce us to bones.

NOTES

The epigraphs for the first section are from Dunya Mikhail's poem "I Was In A Hurry" translated by Elizabeth Winslow and published in her collection *The War Works Hard*, and Ghassan Kanafani's poem, which has been a timely reminder of our need to continue remembering all the children in war-torn countries.

The epigraphs for the second section are from Derek Walcott's collection, *The Star-Apple Kingdom*, published in 1979, and Abdel Wahab Yousif's poem written before he died in 2020 when a rubber boat carrying African immigrants sank into the sea shortly after setting off from Libya on its way to Europe.

The epigraph for the third section is from Nathasha Trethewey's poem, "After Your Death," included in her collection titled *Native Guard*, published in 2006.

The epigraph for the fourth section is from Tarfia Faizullah's poem, "Reading Celan at the Liberation War Museum," included in her collection titled *Seam*, published in 2014.

In "Biography of Homeland," إنالله وينالله راجعون is an Arabic phrase that means "Indeed, to Allah we belong and to Him we will return."

"A Ledger of Losses" is dedicated to the victims of the Nigerian Civil War that happened between 1967-1970, and the victims of the bokoharam insurgency in some of the states in Northern Nigeria.

The epigram for "A Ledger of Losses" is from a poem titled "The Casualties" by J.P. Clark. The poem was first published in his collection of poems titled *Casualties: Poems 1966-68*, published in 1970.

"After the Blasts" is an elegy for the casualties of a blast in northern Cameroon, as reported by *Reuters* on Jan. 9th, 2021.

"The Weight of Leaving" is dedicated to some of the villages affected by terrorism in Northern Nigeria. These villages include Dikwa, Gumna Kayeya, Ilewaya, Keza, Mulfe Balalam, Mafa, and Marte.

"Darak" is dedicated to the victims of the Battle of Darak that occurred on June 9, 2019, when Boko Haram fighters attacked a Cameroonian and MNJTF military base in Darak.

"What Crosses the Sea" is written with gratitude to Naomi Shihab Nye for her poem, "Mediterranean Blue" published in her collection, *The Tiny Journalist* in 2019.

"Requiem at Sea II" is dedicated to the 84 migrants aboard a boat that capsized off the island of El Hierro in the Canary Islands, as reported in *The New York Times*, Sept. 30, 2024.

The epigram for "The Requiem at Sea 1" is from Derek Walcott's *The Sea at Dauphin*, published in 1954.

"Coffins" is an elegy for the victims of the needless attacks from terrorists in Dogon Noma, a community in Kaduna State.

ABOUT THE AUTHOR

RASAQ MALIK GBOLAHAN is a Nigerian poet, performer, translator, essayist, and an emerging DH scholar. The founding Editor-in-Chief of *Agbowó*, he is also a cofounder of *Àtélẹ̀wó*, the first digital journal devoted to publishing literary work written in the Yorùbá language. He is the author of the poetry chapbooks *No Home In This Land,* selected for Chapbook Box edited by Kwame Dawes and Chris Abani, and *The Other Names of Grief,* published by Konya Shamsrumi. His work has appeared or is forthcoming in *POETRY, Ploughshares, Kenyon Review, African American Review, Beloit, Colorado Review, Crab Orchard Review, LitHub, Michigan Quarterly Review, Minnesota Review, New Orleans Review, Prairie Schooner, Poet Lore, Rattle, Salt Hill, Spillway, Stand, Verse Daily,* and elsewhere.

He received Honorable Mention in the 2015 Best of the Net for his poem "Elegy," published in *One.* In 2017, *Rattle* and *Poet Lore* nominated his poems for the Pushcart Prize. He was shortlisted for Brunel International African Poetry Prize in 2017. He was a finalist for Sillerman First Book for African Poets in 2018. His co-edited anthology, *African Urban Echoes,* was published in Spring 2025 by Griots Lounge, Canada. At press time, he was a PhD student at the University of Nebraska-Lincoln. He also was working on a Yorùbá novel and a translation project.

www.ingramcontent.com/pod-product-compliance
Lightning Source LLC
Chambersburg PA
CBHW040009080526
44586CB00028B/2943